Dinner With The King

Communion Dramas
For Youth

Gary W. Fehring

CSS Publishing Company, Inc., Lima, Ohio

DINNER WITH THE KING

Copyright © 2006 by
CSS Publishing Company, Inc.
Lima, Ohio

The original purchaser may photocopy material in this publication for use as it was intended (worship material for worship use; educational material for classroom use; dramatic material for staging or production). No additional permission is required from the publisher for such copying by the original purchaser only. Inquiries should be addressed to: Permissions, CSS Publishing Company, Inc., 517 South Main Street, Lima, Ohio 45804.

Scripture quotations are from the New Revised Standard Version of the Bible, copyright 1989 by the Division of Christian Education of the National Council of the Churches of Christ in the USA. Used by permission.

For more information about CSS Publishing Company resources, visit our website at www.csspub.com or email us at custserv@csspub.com or call (800) 241-4056.

Cover design by Barbara Spencer
ISBN 0-7880-2390-X   PRINTED IN U.S.A.

These dramas are dedicated to the young people of Christ's church who are such welcome and eager participants in our Lord's wonderful gift of himself in the bread and wine of his sacramental meal.

Table Of Contents

Introduction	7
Dinner With The King	9
Passover	21
Jesus Food	29
Partytime	39
Youth Retreat	47
The Evening "Good" News	55

Introduction

These chancel dramas were written to be performed by students in our fifth grade Participation in Holy Communion instruction program. Each was included as the sermon at the Maundy Thursday service of worship during which these young people were welcomed as participants in the Sacrament.

When the dramas were written, a part was included for each member of the class. Each of the dramas should be easily adaptable for any size group. All the dramas reflect the occasion at which they are to be performed as preparation for Holy Communion. As originally performed, the dramas used a minimum of props and costumes. Creative use of both of these would certainly add to the experience of the young people performing them and to the members of the congregation present at the performance.

The "Passover" and "Evening 'Good' News" dramas should be suitable for performance by adults. The "Youth Retreat" drama might be better performed with older youth or adults as the counselors (Person 1 and Person 2).

Dinner With The King

Characters
- Reader
- King
- Servant
- Guests (four, one female)
- Group
  - Poor
  - Sick
  - Lame
  - Number
  - Naked
  - Dead
  - Sinner
  - Lost Sheep
  - Stranger
  - Last Person

Props
- Throne
- Scroll or rolled up paper
- Bell
- Clipboard and pencil
- Labels (for group)
- Wheelchair

Setting

This drama takes place in the front of the sanctuary. The "throne" is placed in the center. The bell, scroll, clipboard, and pencil are placed on the throne. The baptismal font needs to be visible to the congregation.

The Group members need labels so the congregation recognizes them. Costuming is not necessary, but will add to the presentation. These actors are asked to kneel before the King, so make this as comfortable for them as possible.

Reader: *(goes to lectern)* One of the dinner guests, on hearing this, said to him, "Blessed is anyone who will eat bread in the kingdom of God!" Then Jesus said to him, "Someone gave a great dinner and invited many. At the time for the dinner he sent his slave to say to those who had been invited, 'Come; for everything is ready now.' But they all alike began to make excuses. The first said to him, 'I have bought a piece of land, and I must go out and see it; please accept my apologies.' Another said, 'I have bought five yoke of oxen, and I am going to try them out; please accept my apologies.' Another said, 'I have just been married, and therefore I cannot come.' So the slave returned and reported this to his master. Then the owner of the house became angry and said to his slave, 'Go out at once into the streets and lanes of the town and bring in the poor, the crippled, the blind, and the lame.' And the slave said, 'Sir, what you ordered has been done, and there is still room.' Then the master said to the slave, 'Go out into the roads and lanes, and compel people to come in, so that my house may be filled.' " *(sits down)*

(King enters, sits on throne, and rings a bell. Servant enters and bows.)

King: I have decided to have a dinner for my friends. Here is a list of the people I want you to invite. *(hands scroll to Servant)*

Servant: *(takes scroll from the King)* Yes, Your Majesty. *(bows to King then goes to Guest 1)*

Servant: The King has sent me to invite you to the palace next Sunday. He is having a dinner.

Guest 1: What's on the menu?

Servant: Bread and wine.

Guest 1: Any peanut butter?

Servant: No, no peanut butter.

Guest 1: Then tell the King I won't be coming. I never eat bread without peanut butter.

Servant: *(goes to Guest 2 — must be a female)* The King sent me to invite you to the palace next Sunday. He's having a dinner.

Guest 2: Who is going to be there?

Servant: A lot of people.

Guest 2: Like who, for instance?

Servant: Well, I know for certain the King's Son will be there.

Guest 2: Is he cute?

Servant: Not especially.

Guest 2: You better tell the King I won't be there. I never eat with people unless they are as cute as me.

Servant: *(goes to Guest 3)* The King has sent me to invite you to the palace next Sunday. He's having a dinner.

Guest 3: Is he giving away any prizes?

Servant: I suppose, in a way, he is.

Guest 3: Like what?

Servant: Forgiveness of sins, love, peace, joy, hope.

Guest 3: How about big screen TVs? Is the King giving away any big screen TVs?

Servant: I don't think so.

Guest 3: Sorry. I don't need any of that stuff you talked about, but I do need a new television.

Servant: *(goes to Guest 4)* The King sent me to invite you to the palace next Sunday. He's having a dinner.

Guest 4: What King? You mean Elvis is alive?

Servant: I'm not talking about Elvis. I'm talking about your *King*!

Guest 4: I don't have a King. This is America. We did away with kings.

Servant: You didn't get rid of this King. This King is still in business. This country is still part of his kingdom.

Guest 4: For some people this might be his kingdom, but not for me. I don't have a King, and I don't need a King.

Servant: So you won't be coming to the King's dinner?

Guest 4: Not unless the King is Elvis and the dinner is at Graceland.

Servant: Sorry. I can give you "Graceland," but I can't give you Elvis.

Servant: *(reports to King)* Your Majesty, I invited your guests to your dinner, but none of them want to come. To tell the truth, I don't think they are your friends.

King: My Son told me they were his friends. Any friends of his are friends of mine.

Servant: If they are friends of yours, why won't they come to your dinner?

King: They will, when they get hungry enough.

Servant: But, what about next Sunday? We have that big table and no one is going to be there for the dinner.

(Group gathers together in the center of the room)

King: *(points at the group)* I see some people out there. Go and invite them to my dinner.

Servant: But, who are they?

King: Ask them. They will tell you. *(hands clipboard and pencil to Servant)*

Servant: *(Servant goes to Group, bringing along a clipboard and pencil)* The King is having a dinner at the palace next Sunday. There will be bread and wine, no peanut butter. The King's Son will be there and, *no*, he isn't especially cute. There will be free gifts of forgiveness and salvation for everyone. Although the address of the palace is "Graceland," the King isn't Elvis. How many of you would like to be a guest at the King's dinner?

(Group members raise their hands)

Servant: Okay, come forward one at a time so that I can write down your names.

(Poor comes forward)

Servant: Your name, please.

Poor: I am poor.

Servant: Poor? Okay, but do you have a name?

Poor: At last count I had more than two billion names. Is there room for me at the King's dinner?

Servant: You know? There is. The King has this huge banquet table, I never understood why it was so big. I'll bet he planned it that way because he knew you would be coming. *(writes on clipboard)*

(Poor kneels before King; Sick comes forward)

Servant: Who are you?

Sick: I'm sick.

Servant: I can see that. You look terrible. You need a good meal.

Sick: I need more than food.

Servant: The King's meal *is* more than food. We're talking here about the body and blood of Jesus. The best medicine in the universe. *(writes on clipboard)*

(Sick kneels before King; Lame comes forward in wheelchair)

Servant: Who might you be?

Lame: The lame, the blind, the deaf. I can't walk, or see, or hear.

Servant: Can you eat?

Person: I can if I can get to the table. Is it wheelchair accessible?

Servant: Are you kidding? The King invented accessibility. He has this big cross-shaped ramp going right into his banquet hall. *(writes on clipboard)*

(Lame goes to King; Number comes forward)

Servant: What's your name?

Number: Number 69387.

Servant: Who picked out a name like that, your mom or your dad?

Number: The judge. I live in a cell at the state prison.

Servant: Can you get to the King's dinner?

Number: Does he deliver? Domino's Pizza delivers.

Servant: *(shouts to King)* Do you deliver? *(writes on clipboard)*

King: My Son delivers. He is bringing food to prisons all the time.

(Number kneels before King; Naked comes forward)

Servant: Who are you?

Naked: I'm naked.

Servant: No, you're not.

Naked: Not *now*. Give me a break. I'm in a church full of people.

Servant: But, otherwise you would be naked?

Naked: That's right. Do I have to wear clothes to be a guest at the banquet of the King?

Servant: When you come in, the King will give you something to wear. He gives something to wear to everyone who comes to his banquet.

Naked: Is it something nice?

Servant: I'll say. It's the perfect goodness of his Son, Jesus. He made clothes out of it. That's what we all wear when we have dinner with the King. *(writes on clipboard)*

(Naked kneels before King; Dead comes forward)

Servant: Who are you?

Dead: I'm dead.

Servant: So am I. It's been a long day.

Dead: I'm not dead-tired. I'm a dead person. I am all the people of the earth who have died.

Servant: I didn't think dead people ate meals.

Dead: I don't know about that. This is the first meal I have been invited to since I died.

Servant: Well then, since you are invited, the King must want you to come. Are you hungry? *(writes on clipboard)*

Dead: I sure am. Being dead gives a person a real appetite for a meal where the main course is the Bread of Life.

(Dead kneels before King; Sinner comes forward)

Servant: Name, please.

Sinner: I don't know my name. People just call me Sinner.

Servant: Oh ... oh!

Sinner: Oh, oh, what?

Servant: The King gave me a note about you. Here it is. It reads: "Sinner can't come to my banquet unless he takes a bath."

Sinner: A bath? Where?

Servant: *(points to baptismal font)* See that baptism font? That's where you take your bath.

Sinner: Will I fit?

Servant: You'll fit. In baptism, one size fits all. One more thing, after your bath you'll have a new name.

Sinner: What name?

Servant: Saint. At the King's banquet your name tag will read "God's Saint." *(writes on clipboard)*

(Sinner kneels before King; Lost Sheep comes forward)

Servant: Name?

Lost Sheep: Sheep.

Servant: Sheep?

Lost Sheep: That's right, Sheep. L. Sheep.

Servant: And the "*L*" is for?

Lost Sheep: Lost

Servant: So you are the famous Lost Sheep we read about in the Bible?

Lost Sheep: That's me.

Servant: And you would like to go to the King's banquet?

Lost Sheep: Yes, I would. But, I'm lost. How can I find my way there if I'm lost?

Servant: Don't worry. There is a shepherd out there looking just for you. He is going to find you. When he does, he will take you to the palace of the king. *(writes on clipboard)*

(Lost Sheep kneels before King; Stranger has been standing away from rest of Group; Servant calls out to him)

Servant: You over there. Come here.

(Stranger comes forward)

Servant: Who are you, and why are you standing by yourself?

Stranger: I'm alone. I'm a stranger.

Servant: Then, where is your mask?

Stranger: What?

Servant: I thought you said you were the Lone Ranger.

Stranger: I said, I am alone. I am a *stranger.*

Servant: *(uses a "cowboy" accent)* Well then, tell me "stranger," how did you all come to be in these here parts?

Stranger: I just keep moving, but no matter where I go, no one ever invites me in or makes me feel welcome.

Servant: You sure came to the right place today. The King's door is wide open, and he has put out the welcome mat, just for you.

Stranger: But the King doesn't know me. I am a stranger, remember?

Servant: You might be a stranger to the world, but the King knows you. He has always known you. He knew you before you were born. You have never been a stranger to him. You have always been a special friend. *(writes on clipboard)*

(Stranger kneels before King; Last Person comes forward)

Servant: Well, you seem to be the last person. What's your name?

Last Person: Last Person.

Servant: Why doesn't that surprise me? Are you always the last person in every line?

Last Person: That's the way it has been so far. Everyone else pushes their way ahead of me.

Servant: Well, Last Person, I've been given a note about you, too. It says, "Make sure Last Person is first in line for my banquet." It's signed, "The King."

Last Person: This King sure does things in a different way than everyone else.

Servant: Indeed he does! There is a word for it. The word is "Grace." The King calls it "Justice." The King's Son calls it "Love." *(writes on clipboard)*

(Last Person and Servant kneel before King)

King: *(to the congregation)* My banquet hall is being filled, but there is still room at the table for you. All these people are my guests. Join them, and join my Son, at the family meal of his church.

Passover

For freedom Christ has set us free. Stand firm, therefore, and do not submit again to a yoke of slavery.
— Galatians 5:1

Characters
Reader (may be one person reading all three scripture passages or three different people, each reading one passage)
Person 1-6 (six people, may be of either sex, names may be used instead of numbers one through six)

Props
Table and six chairs
Place settings for six
Bowls of food

Setting
A table is placed in the center of the chancel area. The table is set for six. The play opens with five persons sitting at the table. There are bowls of food on the table. The five persons are talking quietly to each other.

Reader: *(goes to lectern)* The LORD said to Moses and Aaron in the land of Egypt: This month shall mark for you the beginning of months; it shall be the first month of the year for you. Tell the whole congregation of Israel that on the tenth of this month they are to take a lamb for each family, a lamb for each household. If a household is too small for a whole lamb, it shall join its closest neighbor in obtaining one; the lamb shall be divided in proportion to the number of people who eat of it. Your lamb shall be without blemish, a year-old male; you may take it from the sheep or from the goats. You shall keep it until the fourteenth day of this month;

then the whole assembled congregation of Israel shall slaughter it at twilight. They shall take some of the blood and put it on the two doorposts and the lintel of the houses in which they eat it. They shall eat the lamb that same night; they shall eat it roasted over the fire with unleavened bread and bitter herbs. Do not eat any of it raw or boiled in water, but roasted over the fire, with its head, legs, and inner organs. You shall let none of it remain until the morning; anything that remains until the morning you shall burn. This is how you shall eat it: your loins girded, your sandals on your feet, and your staff in your hand; and you shall eat it hurriedly. It is the passover of the LORD. *(sits down)*

Person 1: *(runs into the room, shouting)* Hey, Everybody! It's time to go!

Person 2: Don't be in such a hurry!

Person 1: Moses told us we should hurry!

Person 2: We can't go, yet. We haven't eaten.

Person 1: That's right. We have to eat before we go. What's for supper?

Person 2: Roast lamb.

Person 1: Great. I love roast lamb ... but ... the only lamb we own is my pet lamb, Bildad. By the way, where is Bildad? He wasn't in his pen ... Wait a minute ... The roast lamb isn't? ... Oh, no. You couldn't have!

Person 2: We had to. You know that Bildad was a perfect lamb. Bildad was the prettiest, nicest, best lamb our family has ever owned. Moses told us that tonight belongs to God in a very special way. That means that the lamb for our Passover Meal must be a very special lamb. Tonight, God is doing his very best for us. God is ending our old slavery and giving us new freedom. When God does something so special for us, we show our gratitude by doing something special for him. Because God is giving us his best, we give our best. The best we have is Bildad.

Person 1: But I loved Bildad.

Person 2: We all loved Bildad.

Person 1: Why couldn't you have gone to the market and bought a lamb? I know we could only afford the cheapest ones they sell. But we could have kept Bildad.

Person 2: We have a perfect God, who is giving us his best. We can't say, "Thank you," to God with anything less than our very best.

Person 1: I wish you had given me to God instead of Bildad!

Person 2: God would never ask us to sacrifice a child to him. Abraham believed that. So do I. If anyone is going to set slaves free by sacrificing a child, it is going to be God.

Person 1: Would God do that? Would God sacrifice his own child?

Person 2: If that was the only way to set us free, God would. God loves us. God loves us just the way you loved Bildad. You were willing to die so Bildad could live. God would give up his Child, the center of his life, if it was the only way you and I could live.

Person 1: I still miss Bildad.

Person 2: God has promised us a new land, a land of 1,000 hills, each hill covered with sheep. You'll find another lamb.

Person 1: Not like Bildad. Bildad was the best.

Person 2: That's why Bildad had to be our gift to God. Now, sit down and eat. Bildad died to give you strength. You'll need that strength because it is almost time for our freedom journey to begin. Pass ____*(name)*____ the lamb, and the bread, too.

Reader: *(goes to lectern)* The Israelites journeyed from Ramses to Succoth, about six hundred thousand men on foot, besides children. A mixed crowd also went up with them, and livestock in great numbers, both flocks and herds. They baked unleavened cakes of the dough that they had brought out of Egypt; it was not leavened, because they were driven out of Egypt and could not wait, nor had they prepared any provisions for themselves.

The time that the Israelites had lived in Egypt was four hundred and thirty years. At the end of four hundred and thirty years, on that very day, all the companies of the LORD went out from the land of Egypt. That was for the LORD a night of vigil, to bring them out of the land of Egypt. That same night is a vigil to be kept for the LORD by all the Israelites throughout their generations. *(sits down)*

Person 3: What kind of bread is this? It's flat as a pancake, and hard as a rock. Did somebody forget to leaven the dough?

Person 4: We didn't forget. God told us not to do it.

Person 3: Why? Has God made a deal with the dentist? This stuff will break your teeth.

Person 4: Cut it out. It's not that hard. It's just crispy, like a potato chip.

Person 3: Some potato chip, a stale one, without any salt on it, or anything else to give it taste.

Person 4: How it tastes is not important. What is important is that it is, "bread for our journey."

Person 3: What journey?

Person 4: Our journey out of slavery into freedom.

Person 3: Where does this freedom journey start?

Person 4: We start right here.

Person 3: When does it start?

Person 4: We start right now. God doesn't even want us to wait for our bread to rise. We had to bake it without the leaven.

Person 3: So here we are with this flat, tasteless stuff you call bread.

Person 4: It's freedom bread. We don't eat it because it tastes good. We eat it because we need the strength to go where God is sending us, out of slavery into freedom.

Person 3: But it's really hard to chew. I'm afraid it's going to break my teeth.

Person 4: Don't worry about your teeth. Worry about your faithfulness. God has plans for us. Eating this bread will help us live up to the responsibilities of God's gift of freedom. We have some hard work ahead of us.

Person 3: Hard work? I'm used to hard work. I've been a slave all my life.

Person 4: Living in freedom brings with it a different kind of work. Living in slavery requires a strong body. Living in freedom requires a strong soul. That's what this bread is for, to give strength to our souls, strength for doing the hard work of faithfulness.

Person 3: But, I'm telling you, this bread is too dry. I need some wine.

Person 4: Bread and wine. That's a meal that would give us the strength to do just about anything.

Person 3: Anything?

Person 4: Anything God asks; anything our faithfulness to him requires.

Reader: *(goes to lectern)* The LORD spoke to Moses, saying: "Speak to the Israelites, saying: In the second month on the fourteenth day, at twilight, they shall keep it; they shall eat it with unleavened bread and bitter herbs." *(sits down)*

Person 5: Please pass the bitter herbs.

Person 6: You can have them! Yuck!

Person 5: They taste so bad, I kind of like them.

Person 6: Are you nuts? They are supposed to remind us of all the bitter years we have spent as slaves in Egypt. Don't tell me you liked being a slave?

Person 5: Actually, it hasn't been that bad. I work in a nice house. I always have plenty of food. Sometimes I even get to drive the family chariot, a four-horsepower Ramses Special, with ABS and air bags. That's a real set of wheels.

Person 6: But ... you're a slave. You can't go where you want, and you can't do what you want.

Person 5: I don't want to go anywhere, and I don't want to do anything. I'm happy with things as they are.

Person 6: What if God has some place for you to go? What if God has something for you to do? As a slave you would have to pass that up.

Person 5: What could God have that's better than what we've got right here? Sure we're slaves, but we're slaves in the richest country in the world.

Person 6: I suppose you want to die in Egypt.

Person 5: What?

Person 6: I suppose you want to die in Egypt as a slave and a stranger, a person who doesn't really belong, a person who isn't really at home.

Person 5: You make being a slave sound like something bad.

Person 6: It is bad. It is bad because God is giving you freedom as a gift. It's bad to prefer this world's slavery to God's freedom.

Person 5: But what do I get out of being free? What's in it for me?

Person 6: A life where you belong, where you're an insider, not an outsider. A community where no one treats you like a stranger, where everyone calls you friend. A home that's yours forever. A home with God where you can live, and die, and live again, for eternity.

Person 5: That sounds pretty good, but how do I get all that?

Person 6: By letting go of the world that wants to keep you as a slave. By letting go, and grabbing on, grabbing on to God. Just that quick, you're free.

Person 5: You know, these bitter herbs really are awful. Thank God that when our slavery is over, we won't have to eat them anymore.... I wonder what kind of meal God is going to give us while we are living out our freedom?

Person 6: Bread and wine. That's the food slaves eat after God has set them free. Not slavery's bitter herbs, but freedom's bread and wine.

Jesus Food

Characters
　　Person 1-14 (fourteen young people, parts may be adjusted for almost any size group)

Props
　　Table
　　Papers
　　Church directory
　　Two cell phones
　　Notepad
　　Pencil or pen

Setting
　　A table with some papers and a church directory placed on it is in the center chancel area. Where there are blanks for names in the dialogue, they should be filled in with the appropriate names.

(Two young people enter the worship area. They may be talking about anything, such as, what has been happening at school, or what they had been doing the night before. As they reach the table in front, Person 1 searches his/her pockets.)

Person 1: Oh, no!

Person 2: What's the matter?

Person 1: I lost the recipe.

Person 2: Recipe? Recipe for what? You can't cook. If you tried to boil water, you would burn it.

Person 1: I can, too, cook. Last week I cooked a TV dinner. Not just *any* TV dinner, either, a "Hungry Man" TV dinner, an enchilada with spanish rice and refried beans.

Person 2: So the recipe you lost explained all about opening a box and turning on the oven?

Person 1: No! It was a recipe for bread. Remember Pastor _____ read it at communion class? After class I asked him/her for it. I told him/her that I wanted to make the communion bread for our Maundy Thursday service. I put the paper in my pocket. Now I can't find it.

Person 2: Why not ask him/her for another copy?

Person 1: I can't. He/she told me that it was the only copy. He/she told me to be sure not to lose it.

Person 2: And you did. Boy, are you in trouble! They have a special place in hell for people who lose stuff their pastors give them.

Person 1: Hey, don't say that. Jesus will forgive me.

Person 2: But Pastor _____ won't.

(Person 3 comes into the room, joins the pair in front)

Person 2: Hey _____, guess what _____ did. He/she lost Pastor _____'s recipe for communion bread.

Person 3: Really! I hear they have a special place in hell for people who do stuff like that.

Person 1: They do not! Now stop clowning and help me.

Person 3: Help you do what?

Person 1: Help me remember what was in that recipe for communion bread.

Person 3: How can I help you do that? When Pastor _____ was reading it, I was listening to a joke that _____ was telling _____.

Person 2: Was that the joke about the Rice Krispies, the can of Spam, and the band teacher?

Person 3: No, it was the joke about ...

Person 1: *(interrupts)* Stop talking about your stupid jokes and help me remember.

Person 2: We can't. Face it. You were the only one in the whole class listening to Pastor _____ when he/she read that recipe. Why you listened is beyond me. Why would anyone pay attention to a recipe for bread?

Person 1: It wasn't just a recipe for bread. It was a recipe for communion bread, the body of Christ. I thought how neat it would be for Jesus to use the bread I baked and turn it into his body. That would give me a special place in his miracle. Don't you think that's exciting?

Person 2: When you talk about it that way, it really does. I can see why you wanted that recipe.

Person 3: Too bad you lost it!

Person 2: We would help you if we could.

Person 3: But we can't. Sorry.

Person 1: What am I going to do?

Person 3: Running away from home sounds like a good idea, or, joining another church.

Person 1: Stop trying to be funny. You *have* to help me. Remember what Pastor _____ said. We are the body of Christ. The same love we share at communion, we ought to be sharing all week long. You are supposed to love me. If you love me, you have to help me.

Person 2: You make it sound like if we don't help you, we shouldn't take communion.

Person 1: I didn't say that.

Person 3: That's a relief.

Person 1: But the Apostle Paul does.

Person 2: Oh ... Okay ... How can we help?

Person 1: You can tell me what goes into bread.

Person 4: *(enters)* Milk, butter, flour, salt ...

Person 1: What?

Person 4: That's the stuff that goes into bread, I think, that and some other stuff.

Person 3: This isn't just any bread we are talking about. This is communion bread, the body of Christ. What kind of ingredients go into the body of Christ?

Person 2: Let's call some of the other kids in the communion class and see if any of them can tell us.

Person 4: Good idea. I've got my cell phone. I think there is a church directory in that stuff on the table. Bring it over. *(opens the directory)* Let's see ... I'll call _____. *(dials)*

Person 5: *(in another area of the room, answers cell phone)* Hello.

Person 4: Hi, _____, this is_____. A bunch of us are at church and we're trying to find a recipe for communion bread. We need your help.

Person 5: My help? What do I know about communion bread?

Person 4: It's the body of Christ. What would be one ingredient in the body of Christ?

Person 5: God's love. The body of Christ has to be full of God's love.

Person 4: *(to Person 1)* Write down "God's love."

Person 1: *(writes in note pad)* God's love. Got it.

Person 4: Thanks, _____.

Person 2: Let me call _____.

Person 4: Okay, go ahead. You need the directory?

Person 2: No. I know the number. *(dials)*

Person 6: *(now has phone and answers)* Hello.

Person 2: Hi, _____, this is _____.

Person 6: Hi, _____. What's going down?

Person 2: *(names Person 1)* _____ is going down — going down in flames unless we help.

Person 6: What's the problem?

Person 2: It's a long story, but we're over here at church and we're trying to remember what we learned about the body of Christ.

Person 6: The body of Christ? You mean, like communion bread? Well, it's Jesus, our Savior. That's where our salvation is, in Jesus.

Person 2: So there is salvation in the body of Christ?

Person 6: Well, duh ... Didn't you learn anything in communion class?

Person 2: Not much. I didn't think you did, either, you were always telling jokes.

Person 6: Just because I was talking to you doesn't mean that God wasn't talking to me. God has a way of making sure we hear the things he has to say.

Person 2: You're right. I guess I learned that, too, somehow, somewhere.

Person 6: Maybe from Pastor _____.

Person 2: Well ... maybe. Anyway, thanks! *(to Person 1)* Write "salvation" down. _____ says that the body of Christ has a lot of it.

Person 7: *(enters with Person 8, overhears)* A lot of what?

Person 3: Salvation. The body of Christ has salvation in it.

Person 7: I guess the body of Christ has salvation in it. That's what it's all about, salvation.

Person 8: And forgiveness.

Person 7: What?

Person 8: And forgiveness. You were talking about salvation. Salvation and forgiveness go together. Remember what Martin Luther said, "Where there is forgiveness of sins, there is salvation."

Person 7: How do you know what Martin Luther said?

Person 8: Because I listened to Pastor _____, that's how.

Person 7: *(shakes head)* Who said miracles don't happen?

Person 9: *(walks in)* What are you guys talking about?

Person 7: Miracles.

Person 8: Miracles and the body of Christ.

Person 9: That's kind of the same thing, isn't it? The body of Christ *is* a miracle. The body of Christ is full of miracles.

Person 2: *(to Person 1)* Write down "miracles." While you're at it, write down forgiveness, too. Then read us what you've got.

Person 1: God's love, salvation, miracles, and forgiveness. Is that all?

Person 3: Let's check with *(Person 10)* _____. What's the number?

Person 4: Here's the directory. Look it up.

(Person 3 dials)

Person 10: *(with phone, answers)* Bonjour.

Person 3: What?

Person 10: *Bonjour* ... It's French. It means, "Hello." Is this _____?

Person 3: *Si.*

Person 10: What?

Person 3: *Si* ... It's Spanish. It means, "Get a life."

Person 10: Very funny. What's up?

Person 3: We need your help.

Person 10: Who is we?

Person 3: Our communion class. We need to know what's in the body of Christ.

Person 10: I am. So are you. When we were baptized, Christ made us part of his body. I'm a brain. I think you are ...

Person 3: Don't say it. I know what you're thinking and ... don't say it.

Person 10: But ...

Person 3: I asked you not to say it. *(hangs up, to Person 1)* Write down all our names. All of us are in the body of Christ.

Person 1: Okay. You know, this recipe is getting awfully messy.

Person 11: *(enters with Person 12 and overhears)* What's messy?

Person 1: The body of Christ.

Person 11: What's messy about the body of Christ?

Person 12: It's got sinners in it. That makes it messy.

Person 11: The body of Christ has sinners in it?

Person 12: Well ... it's got you in it, hasn't it?

Person 11: Are you calling me a sinner?

Person 12: No, I'm not calling you a sinner.

Person 11: Good.

Person 12: The Bible is.

Person 11: The Bible says I am a sinner?

Person 12: A sinner ... and a saint! You are a sinner who is in the body of Christ. That makes you a forgiven sinner — a saint.

Person 11: Saint *(says own name)* _____. I like the sound of that. So the body of Christ has saints and sinners in it. What a mess. *(to Person 1)* Better add all the names in that church directory to your list. The body of Christ won't be complete without that bunch of saints and sinners.

Person 13: *(enters)* The body of Christ? You guys talking about communion?

Person 1: We need to know what's in the body of Christ.

Person 13: Jesus food.

Person 2: Jesus food?

Person 13: The food Jesus gives us to make his body strong.

Person 2: You mean like "Wheaties"? Like, if we eat "Wheaties" we will get to be champions?

Person 13: The body of Christ we eat at communion is our "Jesus Food," the food Jesus knows will give us the strength to live as God's people.

Person 2: Sounds like Jesus feeds our bodies with his body.

Person 13: And his blood, and all the love of God, all the forgiveness, salvation, and miracles that Jesus brings with him.

Person 1: I give up. There are too many things in the body of Christ to make me a recipe for communion bread. Pastor _____ is going to kill me.

Person 14: *(enters with a box)* Well, here it is!

Person 1: What's that?

Person 14: It's the stuff I got together so we can make the communion bread. Remember, you gave me the recipe. Here it is, by the way. Pastor _____ told you to be sure not to lose it. Well ... what have you guys been talking about?

Partytime

Characters
Person 1-9 (identified by number; could also be adapted for smaller group)

Props
None needed

Setting
Worship area with altar and communion rail (or place to kneel).

(Persons 1 and 2 enter the area from front or side. They walk toward the center aisle area. They are talking together as they walk. The rest of the participants enter from rear or opposite side. They, too, walk toward center aisle area. They are talking together as they walk.)

Person 1: *(calls out to the other group)* Hey! Where are you guys going?

(Groups meet in the center area, a significant distance from the altar)

Person 3: We're going to a party!

Person 2: A party? Where?

Person 3: Just up there. *(points to the altar)*

Person 1: Who is having a party up there?

Person 4: Our best friend.

Person 2: I thought we were your best friends.

Person 4: You are. I should have said our "special friend."

Person 2: Do we know your "special friend"?

Person 5: Maybe. His name is Jesus.

Person 1: You mean that kid who was born on Christmas? Is he still around?

Person 2: I've heard of him. Didn't something happen to him? Wasn't he on the Titanic or something? I heard he died.

Person 6: He did die, but not on a boat. He died on a cross.

Person 2: A cross? How did he get on a cross?

Person 6: People put him there. They nailed him to a cross because they didn't like him.

Person 1: So you are going to a party given by a dead guy who nobody liked? Come on. *(pauses)* Where are you REALLY going?

Person 3: Up there *(points to altar)* to Jesus' party.

Person 2: I thought you said Jesus died.

Person 5: He did die, but now he is alive.

Person 2: *(grabs arm of Person 1)* Come on. Let's get out of here. The next thing these guys will be telling us is that this dead person who nobody liked, and who isn't dead anymore, drinks human blood.

Person 7: No. *We* drink *his* blood.

Person 1: *(loudly)* What?

Person 2: *(pulls on Person 1's arm)* I told you. Let's get out of here!

Person 6: Wait. This is getting all mixed up. Let's start over. First of all, Jesus wasn't a person that "nobody" liked. A lot of people did like him. Jesus was just about the neatest guy who ever lived. He helped people. He cared about everyone, even kids like us.

Person 1: And the cross part?

Person 6: Jesus was too nice. That bothered some people. When they saw how good he was, it reminded them of how bad they were. That's why they didn't like him.

Person 1: Okay. So Jesus was a good guy. But what's this stuff about how he was dead once, but alive now? How did that work?

Person 4: They nailed him to a cross and he died.

Person 1: And?

Person 4: They buried him.

Person 1: And?

Person 4: Three days later God raised him from the dead.

Person 2: I kind of figured that God was going to come into this.

Person 9: Of course, God is going to come into it. Who do you think is able to raise someone from the dead? Arnold Schwarzenegger?

Person 6: Hold it. Let's not get things mixed up again. Where were we?

Person 9: At Easter.

Person 1: Isn't that next Sunday?

Person 6: That's the day we celebrate God raising Jesus from being dead.

Person 2: Why did God take such a personal interest in this Jesus? Was it because Jesus was so good?

Person 6: Partly, but mostly because Jesus was his Son.

Person 1: Jesus was God's Son?

Person 9: You said you knew about Jesus because of Christmas. That's what Christmas is about. The angels and the star and all that. It's all about the baby in the manger being God's Son.

Person 1: I guess I kind of remember hearing about that at Christmas. But, if Jesus was God's Son, how did he die? I thought that is one of those special things about gods. Gods are immortal. That means they don't have to die.

Person 7: Jesus didn't have to die. Jesus chose to die. Jesus loves you and me so much, he chose to die for us. We need friends, right?

Person 2: Right.

Person 7: We need friends to help us along when we are alive, and we need friends to help us along when we die. Jesus chose to be that friend.

Person 5: Because of Jesus we are never alone, not when we live, and not when we die. We always have Jesus to help us, that means we always have God to help us.

Person 7: Jesus chose to join us in our death, so that we can join him in his life.

Person 2: What life? You just said Jesus died.

Person 5: He did die, and then God raised him from the dead. That's Easter. Remember? On Easter, God gave Jesus, his Son, a new and wonderful life. Because of Jesus, God gives that same new and wonderful life to us.

Person 2: Wow! Now let me get this straight ...

Person 4: *(interrupts)* All this is what we talk about every Sunday at church. You should join us. I'm sure our teacher can explain things, and answer your questions, a lot better than we can.

Person 1: Well ...

Person 3: Come on. We've got to get going. We're going to be late for the party.

Person 2: Wait a minute. Not so fast. What about the part where you drink blood? Whose blood?

Person 7: His blood. Jesus' blood. That's what happens at the party. We eat Jesus' body and drink Jesus' blood.

Person 2: Isn't that kind of gross?

Person 1: Sounds like something from a vampire movie.

Person 7: It isn't *human* blood, or part of someone's *human* body. Jesus is God. It is the body and blood Jesus gives us as God. Our God, Jesus, shares himself with us.

Person 1: How does he do that?

Person 7: Jesus shares his body with us when we eat some bread. Jesus shares his blood with us when we drink some wine.

Person 2: Wine? So that's the kind of party it's going to be. Now I see why you're so excited about it.

Person 4: It's only about a teaspoonful of wine. The bread is a round flat thing that tastes like cardboard.

Person 8: We aren't there to pig out. If we wanted to do that we could supersize at McDonald's. We go because it is a special way of being with Jesus, and with each other.

Person 1: Who else is going to be there? Is it a big party?

Person 8: It sure is. People from all over the world are going to be there. God's whole family is there when Jesus gives us his body and blood.

Person 2: God's family? Who belongs to God's family?

Person 5: All God's baptized people.

Person 1: Hey! I was baptized when I was a baby.

Person 2: So was I!

Person 4: Then you're invited to Jesus' party, too. Come on. I'll get the bread.

Person 6: And I'll get the wine.

Person 7: And Jesus will be there.... Like our teacher says, Jesus will be there with forgiveness of sins, life, and salvation.

Person 1: Are you sure it's okay if we come?

Person 8: Jesus would love to have you. So would all of us. That's what Jesus wants God's family to do, love each other, and love to be with each other.

Person 2: What are we waiting for? Let's go.

Person 3: That's what I've been trying to tell you. Come on. It's partytime.

(Group kneels at communion rail)

Youth Retreat

Characters
    Group
        Person 1
        Person 2
        Person 3
        Person 4
    Reader

Props
    Birthday cake
    Table and chairs
    Gift-wrapped Bible
    Party hats

Setting

The Group is gathered in the front of the worship area. There is a table with a birthday cake and a gift-wrapped Bible placed on it. The members of the group are wearing party hats.

The play is written for two counselors (Persons 1 and 2), a Reader (the person who is having a birthday), the Group as a kind of chorus, and two small parts (Persons 3 and 4) within the Group. Names for Group members can be inserted in the appropriate places.

(Persons 1 and 2 enter as Group, gathered around the table, sings "Happy Birthday" to _____.)

Person 1: It's been a great retreat so far, but what are we going to do about food for the party? The only thing we have to eat is that cake.

Person 2: What about the hot dogs?

Person 1: We had them for breakfast.

Person 2: What about the pizza?

Person 1: We ate that with the hot dogs.

Person 2: When did we have the chicken?

Person 1: We ate that with the jelly donuts for snack.

Person 2: Did we eat anything for lunch?

Person 1: Chili and chips, along with sardine sandwiches and hot chocolate.

Person 2: Was that before or after the ambulance came?

Person 1: After. Remember? They had the stomach pump.

Person 2: Oh, yeah. We needed that. When did we eat last?

Person 1: About two hours ago.

Person 2: What did we have?

Person 1: Sloppy joes, hash brown potatoes, tuna hot dish, tacos, cookies, and ice cream.

Person 2: If we ate all that two hours ago, maybe nobody's hungry now.

Person 1: Why don't you ask them?

Person 2: Hey guys, are you hungry?

Group: *(together loudly)* Yes!

Person 2: Won't that cake be enough food?

Group: *(loudly)* No! We're hungry!

Person 2: How about cake and something to drink?

Group: *(loudly)* Okay! But then we want some food!

Person 2: At least we can buy a little time with cake and pop. Do we have any pop?

Person 1: No.

Person 2: Do we have anything to drink?

Person 1: No.

Person 2: Do we have any money to buy anything to drink?

Person 1: No.

Person 2: What happened to all our money?

Person 1: We spent it all when we went bungee jumping.

Person 2: Oh, yeah. That was great.

Person 1: It could have been better.

Person 2: What do you mean?

Person 1: We shouldn't have gone so soon after eating.

Person 2: It did get kind of gross. Remember when ...

Person 1: Let's not talk about it. Okay?

Person 2: But everybody had a good time.

Person 1: Yeah. It's been a great retreat ... so far.

Person 2: What do you mean, "so far"?

Person 1: If we don't feed this crowd, they are going to be pretty upset. _____ probably won't ever speak to you again for ruining his/her birthday party.

Person 2: That's crazy. Look at all the fun everybody's having.

Group: *(sings "Happy Birthday")*

Person 3: It's time for _____ to open his/her present.

Reader: *(opens present)* It's a Bible!

Person 4: Read something.

Reader: On the third day there was a wedding in Cana of Galilee, and the mother of Jesus was there. Jesus and his disciples had also been invited to the wedding. When the wine gave out, the mother of Jesus said to him, "They have no wine." And Jesus said to her, "Woman, what concern is that to you and to me? My hour has not yet come." His mother said to the servants, "Do whatever he tells you." Now standing there were six stone water-jars for the Jewish rites of purification, each holding twenty or thirty gallons. Jesus said to them, "Fill the jars with water." And they filled them up to the brim. He said to them, "Now draw some out, and take it to the chief steward." So they took it. When the steward tasted the water that had become wine, and did not know where it came from (though the servants who had drawn the water knew), the steward called the bridegroom and said to him, "Everyone serves the good wine first, and then the inferior wine after the guests have become drunk. But you have kept the good wine until now." Jesus did this, the first of his signs, in Cana of Galilee, and revealed his glory; and his disciples believed in him.

Person 2: Hey! They had the same problem we have, nothing to drink.

Person 1: Lucky for them Jesus was there. Too bad you didn't invite him here.

Person 2: What do you mean, I didn't invite Jesus here? Of course I did. We all did. Remember what we said...?

Group: *(together, with folded hands and bowed heads)* "Come, Lord Jesus, be our guest. Let these thy gifts to us be blest."

Person 1: You're right. We did invite Jesus. But we still don't have anything to drink.

Person 2: Don't be too sure of that.

Reader: "But those who drink of the water that I will give them will never be thirsty. The water that I will give will become in them a spring of water gushing up to eternal life."

Person 1: So ... thirst isn't a problem for us. But what about food?

Person 2: Listen.

Reader: When it grew late, his disciples came to him and said, "This is a deserted place, and the hour is now very late; send them away so that they may go into the surrounding country and villages and buy something for themselves to eat." But he answered them, "You give them something to eat." They said to him, "Are we to go and buy two hundred denarii worth of bread, and give it to them to eat?" And he said to them, "How many loaves have you? Go and see." When they had found out, they said, "Five, and two fish." Then he ordered them to get all the people to sit down in groups on the green grass. So they sat down in groups of hundreds and of fifties. Taking the five loaves and the two fish, he looked up to heaven, and blessed and broke the loaves, and gave them to his disciples to set before the people; and he divided the two fish among them all. And all ate and were filled; and they took up twelve baskets full of broken pieces and of the fish. Those who had eaten the loaves numbered five thousand men.

Person 1: Jesus makes great wine out of old dish water and feeds 5,000 families with five loaves of bread and two fish ... No wonder you made sure he was invited to our retreat. What kind of meal do you think Jesus has in mind for us?

Reader: Jesus said to them, "I am the bread of life. Whoever comes to me will never be hungry, and whoever believes in me will never be thirsty."

Person 1: I hope what Jesus has to give us is enough for this crew. They are a hungry bunch, that's for sure.

Person 2: I think we can trust Jesus to keep his promises ... Here comes *(birthday person)* _____.

Reader: *(leaves Group and joins Persons 1 and 2)* I want to thank you for this weekend. I'll always remember dropping down on that bungee cord with my stomach full of hot dogs and pizza.

Person 2: None of us will forget that, especially _____. I don't suppose he will ever again stand down at the bottom like that. You should have seen the look on his face when ...

Reader: Anyway, it's been a great retreat and the birthday party was a wonderful surprise. The best part was your present, that Bible. Just reading it makes me feel full, like I had eaten a big dinner. I wonder, would it be okay if I took the cake home? I'm too full to eat any now.

Person 2: What about the rest of the kids?

Person 1: Ask them.

Person 2: Hey, guys, are you hungry?

Group: *(together loudly)* Yes!

Person 2: Then let's go into the chapel. It's time for our Communion Service.

Person 3: All Right! Nobody can fill us up the way Jesus does.

Person 1: One thing, though, before we leave.

Person 2: What's that?

Person 1: No bungee jumping after the service.

Person 2: Why not?

Person 1: With all that food from Jesus inside us, we'll be so heavy we will probably break the cord.

(Everyone leaves together)

The Evening "Good" News

Characters
Danus Ratherus
Shopper 1
Salesman 1
Caesar Augustus
Barbarus Walterus
Member
Shopper 2
Salesman 2
Titus
Censor
Christian
Sinner
Forgiven
Shopper 3
Attila The Hun
Camera operators (nonspeaking)

Props
Table
Microphones (don't need to be operational)
Three video cameras (don't need to be operational)

Setting
A table with microphones for the news anchors, three video cameras, as large as possible, they don't have to work. They can be made from cardboard boxes and tubes. An area with a microphone for the "on the scene" reporters. An area with microphone for the sponsors.

This play is based on the Apostle Paul's first letter to the Church at Corinth. It brings together a typical contemporary news program with the culture of that time.

Danus Ratherus: *(sitting at news table with microphone, camera 1 signals for him to begin)* Hello. From Corinth in ancient Greece, this is your evening news. I am Danus Ratherus and tonight's top story concerns a special meal taking place in a newly formed religious group here in our city, but before we get to that story here is a word from our sponsor.

Shopper 1: *(in sponsor's area)* My chariot has a few spokes missing, and I think it is tiring out my horses a lot sooner than it should. I wonder if it is time to trade it in for a new model?

Salesman 1: Folks, if your chariot isn't cherry anymore, it's time for you to come down here to Charlie's Chariots on Chalk Street just one block from the chairlift to Chicken Avenue. Check Charlie's for the cheapest Chevy chariots this side of China. Don't have the cash? Charlie will cheerfully charge your chariot. Yes, for choice chariots cheap, check with Charlie. Charlie has been in business here in Corinth since the year 0. Listen to what Caesar Augustus had to say:

Caesar Augustus: The bestus chariotus I ever ownedest I gotus from Charlieus.

Shopper 1: Maybe I should buy a chariot from Charlie's. If it's good enough for the founder of the Roman Empire, it's good enough for me.

Danus Ratherus: Welcome back to the news. Leading the news is the story of a dinner being held tonight by a group which, I believe, calls itself "Christians." Our reporter on the scene is Barbarus Walterus. Barbarus, are you there?

Barbarus Walterus: *(in the scene area)* Yes, Danus, I'm here.

Danus Ratherus: Is it true that the members of this new religious group call themselves Christians?

Barbarus Walterus: That's true, Danus. I have been trying to find out what that name means. Here with me I have a member of the group ...

Member: *(interrupting)* A member of the Church!

Barbarus Walterus: What?

Member: Our group is called "Church." I am a member of the Church.

Barbarus Walterus: Why did you choose the name, "Church"?

Member: It describes who we are. We are a people called together by God.

Barbarus Walterus: Which God would that be? Zeus? Apollo? Athena?

Member: The true God. The only God who really is God.

Barbarus Walterus: And that God's name is...?

Member: God!

Barbarus Walterus: Okay ... Well ... Thanks for clearing that up. Danus, I think I am going to try to find someone else who might be a little more helpful.

Danus Ratherus: That's a good idea, Barbarus. But before we get back to Barbarus Walterus and Corinth's new Christian Church, we will have a word from our sponsor.

Shopper 2: (*from sponsor area*) I asked my mechanic about the stains I have been noticing on my garage floor. He told me that my chariot was leaking sap. He said that the seals between the planks were bad and that they would be awfully expensive to fix. I need a new chariot, but I can't afford a year 51 model. I wonder where I can find a used chariot that will be reliable?

Salesman 1: Do you need a different chariot, but don't want to have to sacrifice a whole flock of sheep to buy one? Come on down to Charlie's Used Chariots. This week's special deal is a chariot owned by a little old lady who only drove it to the Coliseum to watch the gladiators kill each other. Remember what Charlie says ...

Salesman 2: Why buy new, when something used will do?

Danus Ratherus: This is Danus Ratherus again and we return you now to Barbarus Walterus. She has with her a member of the newly formed Christian Church which is gathering tonight for what we understand is a very special meal. Go ahead, Barbarus.

Barbarus Walterus: Thanks, Danus. I am here with Titus. Titus is a visitor to Corinth and is to be a special guest at tonight's meal. Titus, what is so special about tonight?

Titus: Tonight is the night in which our Lord was betrayed.

Barbarus Walterus: Your Lord?

Titus: Our Lord Jesus Christ!

Barbarus Walterus: Christ? Is that where the name of your group ...

Titus: Church!

Barbarus Walterus: Sorry. Is that where the name of your church comes from?

Titus: Yes. It comes from our Lord and Savior Jesus Christ. Tonight we eat and drink his ...

Censor: Beep! Beep! Beep! Beep!

Barbarus Walterus: Thank you Mr. Titus. I apologize to the viewers for having to bleep out what Mr. Titus just said. But I have to tell you. It's not something you would want to hear. Not at supper time.

Christian: *(comes to microphone)* Is there a problem?

Barbarus Walterus: Who are you?

Christian: I am a Christian, a member of Christ's Church.

Barbarus Walterus: Could you tell me about this Christ?

Christian: He is God's Son.

Barbarus Walterus: That God would be the God whose name is?

Christian: God!

Barbarus Walterus: That's what I thought. Tell me more.

Christian: This Christ became a human being named Jesus. He was born to share our human life and to sacrifice his perfect life to earn forgiveness for our sins.

Barbarus Walterus: Sins? What are sins?

Christian: Sins are when we do not live the way God created us to live, when we think we know more about how we should live than God does.

Barbarus Walterus: How many people do that?

Christian: Everybody!

Barbarus Walterus: Everybody?

Christian: Ask them.

Barbarus Walterus: Okay. *(holds out microphone to Sinner)* Excuse me. Are you a sinner?

Sinner: You bet. Been one all my life.

Barbarus Walterus: *(holds out microphone to Forgiven)* How about you?

Forgiven: How about me what?

Barbarus Walterus: Are you a sinner?

Forgiven: Does the Emperor Tiberius wear a toga?

Barbarus Walterus: What?

Forgiven: Sure, I'm a sinner. That's the bad news about me. But in Jesus, I am forgiven. That's the good news about me. In our meal tonight, Jesus comes to us to give us an extra gift of his forgiveness.

Barbarus Walterus: You mean Jesus himself is going to be here?

Sinner: He sure is. The risen Jesus has promised to be with us.

Barbarus Walterus: The risen Jesus? What do you mean?

Sinner: Well, the price he paid for our forgiveness was to die for us.

Barbarus Walterus: How?

Sinner: On a cross. Jesus, who never sinned, died a sinner's death on a cross. He did it for us. His death paid the price for the punishment you and I deserve for being sinners. Three days after his death, God, his Father, raised him from the dead. Now Jesus is with God, his Father, in heaven. He is our risen Lord and Savior.

Barbarus Walterus: Danus, are you getting all this?

Danus Ratherus: We sure are Barbarus. What a story! We will get back to you after this commercial message.

Shopper 3: Our chariot was just fine for us when we got married, but now we have a family. There are the twins, Socrates and Aristotle, little Spartacus, and our dog, Spot. If we are going to go anywhere as a family, we need a bigger vehicle. I wonder if Charlie's Chariots has anything that would meet our needs?

Salesman 1: We sure do! Chevy just came out with a new model that actually has four wheels. That's right, folks, four wheels. One in each corner. Just the thing for a growing family. You can get Ma and Pa and all the little tykes right on board. You won't even have to make your mother-in-law walk along behind. Not unless you want to, that is, ha, ha. These new chariots are called SUVs. S is for supersize. U is for ugly as sin. V is for value (which you are not going to get if you buy one of these). But, you know your neighbor is going to get one, so, you better get one first. Listen to what Attila the Hun has to say:

Attila The Hun: If I had one of those SUVs, they wouldn't call me a barbarian.

Barbarus Walterus: I'm back here with the Christians. We have been talking about Jesus Christ, whom they call their Lord and Savior.

Christian: Not just *our* Lord and Savior. Jesus is *your* Lord and Savior, too!

Barbarus Walterus: That's good news because I am beginning to realize that I need one.

Christian: Every sinner does, and every sinner has one. Jesus died for all of us.

Barbarus Walterus: Amen to that! But you said Jesus Christ is going to be here in person tonight. Will I be able to meet him?

Christian: Join us and Jesus will meet you.

Barbarus Walterus: Where?

Christian: In the bread and wine.

Barbarus Walterus: Bread and wine?

Christian: On the night he was betrayed ...

Barbarus Walterus: That's tonight.

Christian: Right. Tonight is the night when Jesus was betrayed. It was on the Jewish Passover.

Barbarus Walterus: I know about that. We have done several stories on the Jewish Passover.

Christian: Jesus and his disciples shared the Passover meal together. During the meal, Jesus washed their feet.

Barbarus Walterus: The Son of God washed people's dirty feet? What was that about?

Christian: It is about being a servant. In his love, Jesus was willing to be a servant to us. We are to have the same love, and express it by being servants to others.

Barbarus Walterus: I like the sound of that. Here in Corinth, we have too many people who want to be served, rather than to serve others.

Christian: It can be that way in the church, too. We all have a lot to learn from our Lord. Thank God, Jesus is with us to help us learn it.

Barbarus Walterus: You keep talking about Jesus being with you. You told me that tonight he is going to be here to meet me. When is that going to happen?

Christian: When we share the communion meal. The bread we share is Jesus' body. The wine we drink is Jesus' blood. As we eat and drink at the meal tonight, the risen Jesus meets us.

Barbarus Walterus: So that's what Titus meant when he said that tonight you eat Jesus' body and drink Jesus' blood. It's bread you eat, and wine you drink.

Christian: And in the meal they come alive with Jesus. Everything that is Jesus is there for us in the communion meal: all his love, all his life, all his goodness, all the forgiveness he has earned for us on the cross. It is all there for us as he meets us in the bread and wine.

Barbarus Walterus: So your meal tonight really is as special as we were told. I would like to join you, if I could.

Christian: Believe and be baptized and Jesus himself invites you.

Barbarus Walterus: With an invitation from him, I am certainly going to be there.

Danus Ratherus: Save a place for me, too, Barbarus. I'm on my way. That's the news for tonight. For once it really is *good* news!

Barbarus Walterus: Amen!